Fervent Prayers

By His Grace I Have Committed Myself To This Assignment

Apostle Stephen A. Garner

Stephen A. Garner Ministries
P.O. Box 1545
Bolingbrook, IL 60440
E-mail: sagarnerministries@gmail.com
www.sagministries.com
ISBN: 978-1541272897

Printed in the United States of America

Table of Contents

Introduction 1
The Arrows Of The Lord 4
Counsel Of The Wicked 7
The Wisdom Of God 10
The Favour Of God 13
Commanding The Winds 16
Reigning In Christ 19
Strongholds Of Confusion 22
Dismantling Destruction 25
Dealing With Strongmen 28
Agents Of Chaos & Confusion 31
Evil Beast 34
Cunning Works 37
Repentance From Dead Works 40
Fear Of The Lord 43
My Stronghold Of Hope 46
Oil Of Gladness 49
The Breaker Anointing 52
The God Who Answers By Fire 55
The Blood Of Jesus 58
Dealing With Serpents 62
The Anointing Of Supply 65
Lust And Evil Appetites 68
Deliverance From The Violent Man 71
Dealing With Family Spirits 74

Table of Contents

Open Heavens   77

Bands Of Wickedness   80

Dethroning Jezebel   83

The Blessings   87

The Kingdom   90

Commanding Your Day   93

Activating The Angelic Realm   96

Soul Destroyers   99

Success Breakthroughs   102

Overcoming Barriers & Progression Blockers   105

The Voice of The Lord   108

INTRODUCTION

Fervent Prayers is written to inspire and ignite your prayer life. I'm a firm believer that the plans of eternity and the counsel of God are always established and enforced in the place of prayer. Throughout the ages, the genesis of heavenly movements were birthed in the earth through men and women who gave themselves continually to the rigors and joys of prayer.

The current trends of global instability and civil unrest that have emerged since the early 2000's are imposing challenges on the well being of the global community. It's during times like these that we can count on our God to manifest Himself and break forth in the earth. He however needs an invitation and our prayers and intercession are the catalyst for this happening. We have entered a time of heightened divine partnerships. You and I are being positioned to shape history and spearhead one of the most phenomenal revivals the earth has ever experienced.

The challenge the Church faces is developing a generation of ministry gifts who will give themselves to the ministry of prayer. Consider the coming of the great revivalist, Christ Himself. There was Anna, a prophet who gave herself to fasting and prayer. There were volumes of prophetic words at stake. The time of fulfillment was at hand. Her prophetic ministry and consistency in prayer was the nexus that joined two worlds or two movements together, which led to a seismic shift in humanity during that time.

The need for Anna type prophets who are committed to intercede is just as important today. These individuals are being crafted, as I write, by the hand of God. They have been hidden in obscurity and hewn out in the quarry for Kingdom exploits. They are people who are fervent in their prayers and igniters of movements that spark revivals globally.

I believe God has given me as well as many of you a charge to co-labor with Christ and raise up a vibrant army of interceding saints. By His grace I've committed myself to this assignment. I trust that you will partner with us and become one who will take responsibility for the affairs of heaven and impose them upon the earth.

James 5:16 KJV
Confess your faults one to another, and pray one for another, that ye may be healed. The effectual fervent prayer of a righteous man availeth much.

This verse provided insight into how fervent prayer works and what can be accomplished when released. Confession of our faults is the catalyst that will lead to the believer moving in the realm of fervent prayer. God is holy and one of the things hell itself loathes is a saint who looks like God in their deeds.

The next thing is to pray for one another so that healing can manifest. The word healed in the referenced verse means to be made whole. There are a plethora of things that have led to people in the Church and the world being broken. It's God's will for people to be made whole.

James further highlights the "Effectual Fervent Prayers" of the righteous availeth much. The Amplified version says, "the earnest heartfelt, continued prayers of a righteous man makes tremendous powerful available, dynamic in its working." So we can gather from this portion of the verse that "Fervent Prayers" release tremendous power that's dynamic or explosive. These kinds of prayers have a very important role in the overall advancement of the Kingdom as they have direct impact on the believer and the conditions they are in.

The word fervent literally means to be operative, be at work, put forth power, to work for one and aid one. This book is comprised of prayers tailored to manifest power and aid the believer. I encourage you to pray them daily and trust God to manifest His ability on your behalf and those you target in prayer. May heavenly portals open over you and supernatural encounters propel you forward is my prayer!

Apostle Stephen A. Garner

CHAPTER 1

THE ARROWS
OF THE LORD

Thine arrows are sharp in the heart of the king's enemies; whereby the people fall under thee.

Psalm 45:5

1) I declare the arrows of the Lord are against all enemies of righteousness in Jesus Name.

2) Lord arise and activate Your holy archers in my life to shoot forth Your arrows of deliverance and justice on my behalf.

3) I decree inaccuracy on all archers of wicked arrows assigned against me and my family.

4) Lord cause Your hand to manifest against every arrow of injustice loosed against my life in Jesus Name.

5) I take up the shield of faith and decree every fiery arrow of darkness against my health, prosperity and Kingdom mandate is quenched in Jesus Name.

6) I decree the arrows of The Lord Sabaoth are sharpened and accurately aligned against all mine enemies.

7) Lord loose Your arrows against all powers, programs, plans and purposes of devils aligned against me in Jesus Name.

8) I declare the arrows of Your deliverance are upon all adversarial forces. As the prophet Elisha gave command to loose them.

9) Lord cut off the archers of Babylon. Let not their arrows of confusion be released against me.

CHAPTER 2

COUNSEL OF THE WICKED

Psalm 64:2 (KJV)
Hide me from the secret counsel of the wicked;
from the insurrection of the workers of iniquity:

1) Lord release me from every strategy and systematic scheme of darkness set against me.

2) I renounce every secret agenda of dark things programmed against me.

3) I decree every obstruction of darkness hidden from me is exposed by fire in Jesus Name.

4) Father, manifest Your light and judgment upon every work of insurrectionist employed against me.

5) I command impotency upon all deeds of corrupt counsel that would be released into my purpose.

6) Arise and discomfit the counselors of unjust and unrighteous works seeking to infiltrate the destiny of me and my family in Jesus Name.

7) I claim refuge from all illegal maneuvers and actions taken by insurrectionist against my purpose in the earth.

8) I decree the words and counsel of the wicked shall not be established nor take root in my life.

9) Divine disruption comes upon every initiative taken for my demise both naturally and spiritually by wicked counsel in Jesus Name.

10) I loose confusion and dissension on the plans of the wicked against me and my family in Jesus Name.

11) Fire and brimstone rain down upon all strongholds of darkness disseminating evil and unrighteous counsel into my sphere and territorial grid. I decree those voices are cut off by fire in Jesus Name.

12) Lord arise and deliver my soul from all enemies positioned in my pathway that would take counsel together against my soul. Destroy their confederacies and don't let their plans be established.

13) Lord bring the counsel of the heathen to naught that would seek to divert us from heavens agenda. Let not the voice of evil speakers prevail in Jesus Name.

14) I declare Your counsel stands forever and that of wicked counselors perish at Your presence.

15) Your great counsel and mighty works shall withstand. Your rewards break forth and You recompense the fruit of my doing in the earth Jesus Name.

CHAPTER 3

THE WISDOM OF GOD

Luke 2:52 KJV
And Jesus increased in wisdom and stature, and in favour with God and man.

1) Lord I yield to Your wisdom and decree increase daily.

2) Every agenda of foolishness is divinely overturned and dismantle by the wisdom of God.

3) I loose your wisdom over my life and I decree every demonic assignment employed against me comes to naught in Jesus Name.

4) I proclaim wisdom over every endeavor I put my hands to in Jesus Name.

5) Lord as Solomon excelled in wisdom I decree I to excel in wisdom.

6) I proclaim that Your wisdom strengthens me and understanding is causing my days to be lengthened in Jesus Name.

7) By Your wisdom I access the realm of witty ideas and invention. Every creative blocker be bound in Jesus Name.

8) Grace is upon me to build effectively in all relationship, health, business and financial matters by the wisdom of God.

9) I proclaim Your wisdom is the principal thing in my life.

10) I receive sound wisdom as my inheritance. I decree it's laid up for me and my children's children throughout all generations in Jesus Name.

CHAPTER 4

THE FAVOUR OF GOD

Exodus 3:21 KJV
And I will give this people favour in the sight of
the Egyptians: and it shall come to pass, that,
when ye go, ye shall not go empty:

1) Every worlds power and structure seeking to forbid me access to higher places are overthrown by the favour of God.

2) Lord as favour was upon Israel to exit Egypt with substance, I decree my exodus from all limitations manifest by Your favour upon me in Jesus Name.

3) Preserving power and abundance manifest by Your visitation and favour upon me.

4) I decree every contract with lack in my life is void and obsolete because of Your favour.

5) I loose Your favour over my life and command all cycles of delay and setbacks to be broken in Jesus Name.

6) Every negative and unfavorable plot against my purpose is overturned by favour.

7) I prophesy Your shield of favour deals with all demonic darts, arrows and projectiles assigned against my promotion in Jesus Name.

8) I decree that through my intercession Your favour goes before me and prevails in Jesus Name.

9) By You, my faith, family, future and finances stand strong. I decree this in Jesus Name.

10) Front of the line passes, preferential treatment and preferred status are my portion because of Your favour upon my life.

CHAPTER 5

COMMANDING THE WINDS

Ezekiel 37:9 KJV
Then said he unto me, Prophesy unto the wind,
prophesy, son of man, and say to the wind, Thus
saith the Lord God ; Come from the four winds, O
breath, and breathe upon these slain, that they
may live.

1) Lord release a fresh impartation for prophecy, prophetic ministry and prophetic acts upon my life.

2) I prophesy movement upon every area of stagnation in my ministry, business and mandates in life.

3) I command the winds of God to blow upon my destiny in Jesus Name.

4) I decree the winds of God destroy every structure of failure seeking to demolish my house, vision and purpose in Jesus Name.

5) I command all satanic winds blowing to cease.

6) The peace of God overpowers every wind of destruction and chaotic works employed against me.

7) I prophesy to the winds of life and command them to flow upon all who come from my loins both naturally and spiritually.

8) I decree the winds of God scatter all adversity and strongholds of evils aligned against my mission in Jesus Name.

9) I command the power of God to flow in all my affairs by the south winds. Blow south winds, blow in Jesus Name.

10) I decree the east winds of the Lord are destroying every demonic crop in my life.

11) All sanctions and impositions of injustice are displaced by the west winds. I command you to blow upon lack, poverty, confusion and error in Jesus Name.

12) I command the north winds to drive away the rains of the wicked that seek to flood my life in Jesus Name.

CHAPTER 6

REIGNING IN CHRIST

Romans 5:21 KJV
***That as sin hath reigned unto death, even so
might grace reign through righteousness unto
eternal life by Jesus Christ our Lord.***

1) The reign of every sin, proclivity and
   generational bondage is now dethroned in
   Jesus Name.

2) I decree all high places of darkness that have
   reigned over me and subjected me to torment,
   destruction, sickness and poverty are under
   my feet in Jesus Name.

3) I decree I'm seated and reigning in heavenly
   places in Christ Jesus.

4) The grace of the Lord has positioned me to
   reign in life and over all life's circumstances.

5) I decree I reign in Christ over all witchcraft
   and seductive forces in Jesus Name.

6) I decree I will not die before my appointed
   time. Premature death is neutralized and
   rendered ineffective in Jesus Name.

7) I renounce all plans to bring my marriage,
   ministry and mandate to ruins. I decree by
   Your grace and the gift of righteousness, I
   reign in Christ.

8) Lord You've declared if I suffer with You I will reign with You.

9) I renounce all works of hypocrisy and decree they shall not reign over me in Jesus Name.

10) I decree Your reign over my realm and sphere of influence. Every enemy sent to cut off my mandate of success is subdued in Jesus Name.

11) I proclaim divine alignment in every area of my life, I decree every demonic force deployed against my connectivity in Christ is neutralized by the blood of Jesus.

12) Every dark power operating to destabilize and distract me from the purpose of God in Christ are destroyed in Jesus Name.

13) Lord cause me to rise in You and become that vessel of wisdom, righteous, sanctification and redemption to my generation in the Name of Jesus.

14) Every appointment of death and destruction is subdued for I am made alive in Christ by the power of God.

15) I decree that in Christ I reign over the powers of darkness, excel in my calling and live triumphantly in living for Christ all my days.

CHAPTER 7

STRONGHOLDS OF CONFUSION

Isaiah 24:10 (KJV)
The city of confusion is broken down: every house
is shut up, that no man may come in.

1) I renounce every combative force of confusion assigned against my mind and mental wellbeing in Jesus Name.

2) Lord clothe me with Your peace and blot out the works of confusion.

3) I decree clarity and divine focus from start to finish for all assignments and mandates ordained for me.

4) I loose frustration and vexation from the Lord against all mind binding spirits in Jesus Name.

5) Lord, release fires of judgment upon all spirits of mind control and confusion.

6) Lord release Your peace over my thoughts and cause me to walk stable before You in Jesus Name.

7) Father deliver me from the three fold cord of envy, strife, confusion and the evil it would seek to loose upon me in Jesus Name.

8) All the cohorts of confusion are destroyed by fire in Jesus Name.

9) Father release shame and confusion upon all powers advocating my demise in Jesus Name.

10) My trust is in You Lord. Let me never be put to confusion.

11) Release your hammer to break down every assignment of confusion designed against my house. All points of entry are denied and cutoff in Jesus name.

CHAPTER 8

DISMANTLING
DESTRUCTION

Psalm 35:17 KJV
Lord, how long wilt thou look on? rescue my soul
from their destructions, my darling from the
lions.

1) I renounce every destructive force of darkness assigned against me through my blood line and territorial powers in Jesus Name.

2) Lord arise in me and destroy every agenda, seed and strongman of destruction.

3) Lord manifest Your fire and burn all cords of destruction at work against my soul.

4) I renounce all mindsets, behavior patterns and habits that serve as source destructive cycles in my life.

5) I decree every force of darkness aligned against my destiny and purpose is overthrown in Jesus Name.

6) I renounce all cycles of destruction programmed against my health, finances, family and faith.

7) All works of destruction, working to root out my increase, are bound. I forbid your works in Jesus Name.

8) I decree the destructive plans of darkness have come to a perpetual end and vicious cycles are eternally banned in my life.

9) I decree pits of destruction await all dark powers sent against me and my family in Jesus Name.

10) Lord You alone redeem my life from destruction and crown me with Your tender mercies and loving kindness.

CHAPTER 9

DEALING WITH STRONGMEN

Luke 11:21-22 KJV
When a strong man armed keepeth his palace, his goods are in peace: 22 But when a stronger than he shall come upon him, and overcome him, he taketh from him all his armour wherein he trusted, and divideth his spoils.

1) I renounce all strongholds and strongmen assigned against me in Jesus Name.

2) Lord empower me to come out and break fellowship with all devils governing strongholds in my life in Jesus Name.

3) Lord spoil the works and tactics of strongmen working for my demise.

4) I decree all roots of the affects of strongholds are burned by fire in Jesus Name.

5) All strongholds employed to subdue me and pervert my future are neutralized by the blood of Jesus.

6) All strongmen propagating deception and error are cut asunder by the sword of the Lord.

7) I loose Your glory upon all illegal works and sanctions connected to blood line strongmen in Jesus Name.

8) Lord break in and set me free from strongholds working with territorial strongmen plotting my failure and destruction in Jesus Name.

9) All traps, pits, ensnarements and demonic containers holding my name and future guarded by strongmen are overturned by the blood of Jesus.

10) I decree all demonic laws and statues activated against me, by blood line strongmen, causing addictions and destructive behavior patterns are broken in Jesus Name.

CHAPTER 10

AGENTS OF CHAOS AND CONFUSION

1 Corinthians 14:33 KJV
For God is not the author of confusion, but of peace, as in all churches of the saints.

1) I fall out of agreement with all agents of chaos and confusion in Jesus Name.

2) Lord unravel and overthrow all structures governing works of confusion.

3) I prophesy to the winds and command them to blow up all works of chaos.

4) I decree all systems and agents of chaos loosed against my faith, family and finances are overwhelmed and driven out in Jesus Name.

5) Lord arise as the Prince of Peace and destroy the works of confusion in Jesus Name.

6) I loose clarity and peace over my mind and thoughts in Jesus Name.

7) Lord deliver me from all chaos and confusion that accessed me through unwholesome connections and unrighteous works in Jesus Name.

8) I invoke Your fire to burn all bands of confusion and toxic mindsets seeking to cause confusion and chaos in my life.

9) Every cord and tentacle of the demon spirit of mind control is bound and severed by the sword of the Lord.

10) All psychic activity, working against my soul to manipulate my destiny by works of confusion and chaos, are rooted out of me in Jesus Name.

CHAPTER 11

EVIL BEAST

Leviticus 26:6 KJV
And I will give peace in the land, and ye shall lie down, and none shall make you afraid: and I will rid evil beasts out of the land, neither shall the sword go through your land.

1) Father release Your judgments upon all evil beast working against me to secure my demise in Jesus Name.

2) I renounce all fear, panic, anxiety and terror resulting from demonic forces operating as evil beast in my home and health.

3) I receive Your peace which surpasses all understanding. I decree I lie down in rest and nothing can make me afraid.

4) Lord arise and break the sword of the wicked sent against my destiny in Jesus Name.

5) I invoke the benefits of Your covenant of peace with me and I receive deliverance from the works of evil beast in Jesus Name.

6) Every entity, program and system warring against my breakthrough by evil beast are bound in Jesus Name.

7) I renounce all evil beast sent into my life as false apostle, false prophets and false teachers. I decree you are bound in Jesus Name.

8) I decree deliverance by fire from all demonic ground troops sent into my life as evil beast.

9) I decree the Spirit of burning and judgment descends upon all strongholds and hiding places of evil beast positioned for my destruction.

10) Every demonic spirit that would seek to manifest as an evil beast of bad news is overthrown and destroyed by the sword of the Lord.

11) Evil beast employed against me to place false burdens on me succumb to the power of God.

12) All intimidating beast in the market place seeking to devour my increase and cut off the path ways for my success are bound and burned by fire in Jesus Name.

CHAPTER 12

CUNNING WORKS

Exodus 31:3-4 KJV
And I have filled him with the spirit of God, in wisdom, and in understanding, and in knowledge, and in all manner of workmanship, 4 To devise cunning works, to work in gold, and in silver, and in brass,

1) Lord I receive an impartation of wisdom, understanding and knowledge for cunning works.

2) I proclaim divine deposits of inspiration flow through me regularly for supernatural works.

3) Lord release insight into my life that will foster cunning works to glorify You in Jesus Name.

4) Lord I decree that by Your wisdom, skillful works prevail in my life and bring me into renewed prosperity.

5) I prophesy the manifestation of cunning works being birthed in me for the advancement of the Kingdom.

6) I receive wisdom and understanding for cunning works to lead my family into paths of righteousness.

7) I proclaim a continual times of refreshing over my life releasing understanding for cunning works of dominion in Jesus Name.

8) I command portals of creativity to open over my mind.

9) I speak creative surges of divine strategies for success, wealth and prosperity flow within.

10) Credible gains and high levels of productivity are upon. My mind is a hub for inspired works in Jesus Name.

11) Lord sharpen me by Thy Word and in my inward parts cause me to know wisdom and inspire me to devise cunning works in Jesus Name.

12) I receive a fresh baptism for inspired works and I decree doors of elevation and promotion open unto me.

CHAPTER 13

REPENTANCE FROM DEAD WORKS

Hebrews 6:1 KJV
Therefore leaving the principles of the doctrine of Christ, let us go on unto perfection; not laying again the foundation of repentance from dead works, and of faith toward God,

1) Lord expose all dead works established against my destiny and calling, by Your fire destroy them in Jesus Name.

2) I come out of agreement with all dead works rooted in religion, carnality and background dysfunctions.

3) I repent of all fleshly vices I've allowed to control my desires and appetites that have birthed dead works in Jesus Name.

4) I repent of all hereditary bondages that promote fruitless activity in my life.

5) I repent of all mindsets and mentalities that promote dead works in my faith in Jesus Name.

6) Every dead work that has subjected me to hardships, poverty and despair is neutralized in Jesus Name.

7) I decree a fresh anointing upon me to triumph over dead works and the cycles they have produced against me.

8) I decree the power of repentance liberates me from all dead works established to drive me to ruin and failure.

9) I renounce all strongholds and strongmen seeking to control me through dead works in Jesus Name.

10) I receive empowerment from the Lord to rise victoriously over every pattern of dead works in Jesus Name.

11) Lord I repent of any stagnation, inactivity and slothfulness subtly at work to minimize my impact and contribution to humanity in Jesus Name.

12) Lord You alone are the resurrection and the life. Resurrect me from all dead works that have confined me to low places in Jesus Name.

CHAPTER 14

FEAR OF
THE LORD

Proverbs 1:7 KJV
The fear of the Lord is the beginning of knowledge: but fools despise wisdom and instruction.

1) Wells of knowledge and insight are active in me and foolishness suffers severe drought by the fear of the Lord.

2) I renounce all agendas, agencies, systems and programs of foolishness that would lead me to model irreverent behavior in Jesus Name.

3) I decree that Your mercy and truth are purging me of all iniquity and the fear of the Lord breaks all cycles of evil in Jesus Name.

4) Every besiegement of lack and insufficiency is displaced. There is no lack to those who fear the Lord.

5) I decree all issues of my heart that hinder progression in Christ are now perfected by the fear of the Lord.

6) Wisdom to excel and succeed prevail mightily in my life by the fear of the Lord.

7) I renounce all impurities, uncleanness and works of defilement and I decree I'm clean by the fear of the Lord.

8) Father reveal Your secrets and make known Your plans to me as the fear of the Lord increases in my life in Jesus Name.

9) Angelic reinforcements prevail in my life and encircle my entire household by the fear of the Lord.

10) I decree divine levels of disdain for pride, arrogance and the evil way by the fear of the Lord.

11) Cause Your secrets and counsel to openly thrive in my life by the fear of the Lord.

12) I decree advanced knowledge and supernatural insight flow strongly within me by the fear of the Lord.

13) The fear of the Lord is clean and I receive cleansing from all contaminates of darkness in Jesus Name.

14) Prolonged life and length of days are upon me by the fear of the Lord.

15) The snares of death are neutralized and the fountains of life burst open by the fear of the Lord.

CHAPTER 15

MY STRONGHOLD
OF HOPE

Psalm 71:5 KJV
For thou art my hope, O Lord God: thou art my trust from my youth.

1) Lord You alone are my hope and my trust is rooted in You.

2) I decree every generational flow of iniquity bent on perverting me and shifting my life into confusion is over powered by my hope in You.

3) Lord cause the works of all hypocrites and hypocrisy to perish because I hope in You.

4) I receive strength in my heart and courage to excel because I hope in You.

5) Counsel and secret insight into issues plaguing me are manifesting now because I hope in Your mercy.

6) Every dark power sent to sow depression and discouragement are subdued because I hope in You.

7) Salvation, healing, deliverance and access to miracles are mine because I hope in Your word.

8) All sorrow and torment are displaced from my destiny and my hope in the King is loosing gladness.

9) Double blessing, double portions and double breakthroughs are mine for I am a prisoner of hope.

10) Grace to advance and peace to increase prevails because my soul waits and hopes in God alone.

11) Every demonic fire ignited to root out my hope by tragedy, trauma and trials die and its flames come to naught in Jesus Name.

12) I decree every seed of hopelessness, sown against me, experiences severe crop failure in Jesus Name. You alone are the hope of my salvation.

13) I receive an abundance of hope and comfort without fail by the Word of God.

14) Every prophetic word, declared over me, is a constant source of hope and all other words, not inspired by You, fall to the ground and perish in Jesus Name.

CHAPTER 16

OIL OF GLADNESS

Hebrews 1:9 KJV
Thou hast loved righteousness, and hated iniquity; therefore God, even thy God, hath anointed thee with the oil of gladness above thy fellows.

1) Love for righteousness and hatred for iniquity prevails and the oil of gladness flows upon me.

2) I decree the oil of gladness is releasing a fresh anointing over me for elevation out of sorrow and brokenness in Jesus Name.

3) Manifestations of strength and honor are surging within me and gladness of heart overwhelms me abundantly.

4) Lord by Your power put gladness in my heart and empower me to breakthrough every barrier of sorrow.

5) Every cycle of mourning programmed against me breaks and by Your glory I'm girded with gladness in Jesus Name.

6) I decree that by the righteousness of God, light breaks through darkness and gladness moves mightily in my heart.

7) By Your fire, cut off every expectation of the wicked and cause my hope to draw me into gladness.

8) Let the oil of gladness destroy every yoke of distress and root any hidden depression out of me in Jesus Name.

9) I renounce every bondage orchestrated by the powers of darkness to rob me of joy and contentment in Jesus Name.

10) I decree the strongmen over pits, snares and plots to bring me into a low place are destroyed by the oil of gladness upon my life in Jesus Name.

CHAPTER 17

THE BREAKER ANOINTING

Micah 2:13 Young's Literal Translation
Gone up hath the Breaker before them, They have broken through, Yea, they pass through the gate, Yea, they go out through it, And pass on doth their king before them, And Jehovah at their head.

1) I prophesy renewed strength for breakthrough for the Breaker has gone before me.

2) I command gates of resistance to the flow of wealth and prosperity to now be dismantled and broken in the Name of Jesus.

3) Every generational proclivity and active breaks of my family line have been destroyed because the Breaker, has risen in the midst.

4) Mindsets and mentalities of lack that have ruled are now broken in the Name of Jesus.

5) I decree the anointing of breakthrough flows upon me and I breakthrough in every assignment ordained for my life.

6) I renounce all pessimism and demonic tendencies that would release uncertainties regarding all ordained breakthroughs in Jesus Name.

7) Every satanic plot and evil strategy working to undermine my advancement and access to the new levels of visibility and influence, I command you to be broken by the hammer of the Lord and burned by His fire in Jesus Name.

8) Every foundation laid in my bloodline vowed to poverty, failure, ignorance and destruction is now broken up because the Breaker has gone before me.

9) I speak breakthrough over every business endeavor I put my mind, hands, time and resources to in Jesus Name.

10) I proclaim generational breakthrough over my children and my children's children. The breaker has gone up before them and they experience glory after glory after glory in Jesus Name.

CHAPTER 18

THE GOD WHO ANSWERS BY FIRE

1 Kings 18:24 KJV
And call ye on the name of your gods and I will
call on the name of the LORD: and the God that
answereth by fire, let him be God. And all the
people answered and said, It is well spoken.

1) Lord I call upon Your name today and ask that
    You deliver me by fire.

2) I receive Your pillar of fire to burn at night
    over me and my family.

3) I command enemy combatants sent to ensnare
    and seduce me, from my purpose, to be gulfed
    by the fire of God.

4) Lord as You answered Elijah by fire and
    destroyed the false prophets of Baal so let it be
    in my life where every voice of error,
    deception, seduction, bewitchment and
    control are burned by fire.

5) As You spoke to the prophet Moses by fire
    from the burning bush so let Your word
    manifest unto me like fire.

6) I receive fire upon my life to ignite me to
    teach, preach, prophesy, flow in miracles,
    signs and wonders in Jesus Name.

7) I prophesy a renewal of the fires of love for
    You and holiness unto You burning strong
    within me.

8) Let there be a purifying by the fire of God upon every area of my life in Jesus Name.

9) I loose Your fire to go before me and consume with vengeance spirits of poverty, carnality, compromise and fear in Jesus Name.

10) All cords, ties, connections and chains orchestrated to restrict my movement are burned by the fire of the Lord.

11) Let Your Word be like fire shut up in my bones, igniting me to prophesy and proclaim Your Word with great boldness and demonstrations in Jesus Name.

12) I decree a fresh fire burns within me to advance Your Kingdom and fulfill the great commission through my calling in Jesus Name.

CHAPTER 19

THE BLOOD
OF JESUS

Zechariah 9:11 KJV
As for thee also, by the blood of thy covenant I have sent forth thy prisoners out of the pit wherein there is no water.

1) Deliverance from pits and low places of life is manifesting by the blood covenant I have in Christ.

2) I prophesy freedom from every stronghold activated to limit me and every prison designed to confine me by the blood of Jesus.

3) Every area of my mind is liberated from the damning affects of sin, iniquity and curses by the blood of Jesus.

4) The blood of Jesus purges my conscience from every dead work. My mind and thoughts shall glorify the Lord.

5) By the blood covenant I have with Christ all strongholds and strongmen of bitterness, strife and unforgiveness are neutralized and rendered ineffective in Jesus Name.

6) Every sickness imposed upon me by genetic disorders and hereditary strongholds of infirmity break today through the blood of Jesus.

7) All demonic activity in my body responsible for any and all underlining health issues are rooted out by blood and fire in Jesus Name.

8) I decree I scale every wall, breakthrough every partition and rise above every hedge by the blood of Jesus, for His blood gives me access to God.

9) I decree all legal holds of sin; guilt and condemnation are dissolved and eternally displaced from my life by the blood of Jesus.

10) All demonic contracts and assignments of destruction are overthrown and subjugated by the blood of Jesus.

11) The blood of Jesus supersedes and superimposes all generational assignments of wickedness, failure, injustices and evil tendencies.

12) The blood of Jesus is speaking better things on my behalf and overrides every voice of my background and family line propagating small mindedness and mediocrity in Jesus Name.

13) Sanctification and righteousness excel in my members by the blood of Jesus.

14) I decree my ministry, mantle, mission and mandate are genetically coded by the blood of Jesus to bring dead things to life.

15) I decree a blood covering over my dwellings, place of business, pathways of travel, activities and movements by the blood of Jesus.

CHAPTER 20

DEALING WITH SERPENTS

Luke 10:19 KJV
Behold, I give unto you power to tread on serpents and scorpions, and over all the power of the enemy: and nothing shall by any means hurt you.

1) Serpent and scorpion crushing power abides in me.

2) I decree all serpents employed against me are burned by and consumed by the fire of God.

3) I shake myself loose from all serpents that have latched on to my marriage, money, ministry and mandate in Jesus Name.

4) I renounce the allurement and seductive works of serpents of lust and perversion sent to defile me and destroy my purpose in Jesus Name.

5) I receive an anointing for peace to crush serpent powers active to rob me of rest and wholesome living in Jesus Name.

6) I renounce the spirit of Nahash (serpent) sent to obstruct my vision and seduce me in covenants not ordained by God.

7) I decree redemptive power flows to liberate me from all serpents that have caused the eyes of my mind to become impaired.

8) Lord heal me from all mind binding and mind blinding serpents sent by the god of this world.

9) I renounce any venomous serpents working to loose poison and deadly toxins into covenant relationships in Jesus Name.

10) I renounce every python spirit sent by hell to cut off the flow of love, power, anointing, wisdom and increase in Jesus Name.

11) I loose fire upon all constricting serpents in Jesus Name.

12) All works of grief and spiritual vexation, working with Python, is bound in Jesus Name.

13) Python spirits sent to minimize my pursuit of God and restrict me spiritually are cut asunder by the sword of the Lord.

14) Every witchcraft spirit working with the serpent of python I ask You to expose and judge, Lord.

15) All entanglements with the world and carnality connected to the serpent of python are disengaged and displaced from my life by the spirit of burning in Jesus Name.

CHAPTER 21

THE ANOINTING
OF SUPPLY

Philippians 1:19 KJV
For I know that this shall turn to my salvation through your prayer, and the supply of the Spirit of Jesus Christ,

1) All works of insufficiency are rooted out of my life and a supply of the Spirit manifest to appease every need in Jesus Name.

2) I renounce all demonic agencies of darkness working against me to cut off supply lines of provisions.

3) I decree that I have sufficiency in all things by the supply of the Spirit of Jesus Christ.

4) I prophesy a supply of sufficient capacity to deal with all opposition operating against me.

5) Fire and judgment flow from Your throne upon every enemy of supply.

6) Lord expose every plan of darkness to sabotage my supply of increase in Jesus Name.

7) I receive a sufficient supply of Your Spirit for continual breakthrough and marital harmony in Jesus Name.

8) Every force of darkness striving against the increase and sustainability of my family comes to ruin and we thrive by the supply of the Spirit of Christ.

9) Healing, deliverance, miracles and breakthrough supply my life daily in Jesus Name.

10) Streams of creativity for finances, abundance and wealth are being supplied to me in my dreams and by way of revelation.

11) I renounce all siege warfare against my harvest and command any demons assigned against my supply lines to be bound in Jesus Name.

12) I decree every demonic confederacy blocking my increase is divinely displaced and neutralized by the power of the blood of Jesus.

CHAPTER 22

LUST AND EVIL
APPETITES

Psalm 106:14 KJV
But lusted exceedingly in the wilderness and tempted God in the desert.

1) I renounce all lust, evil appetites, designs and passions imposed upon me through generational proclivities.

2) Lord by fire purge me from all evil inhibitions set up to defile me and put my destiny on a collision course of destruction.

3) I proclaim deliverance from all evil tendencies and the temptations rooted in them to drive a wedge between God and me.

4) Lord empower me to elevate my sight and rise higher in my desire for You.

5) Every demonic territorial portal open over me releasing lust and perversion, I command to be closed in Jesus Name.

6) Grace and disciplines to crucify evil appetites increase in me daily.

7) All evil dreams and raiders of the night are forbidden from any access to my place of rest. I decree a wall of fire around my dwelling in Jesus Name.

8) My mind is kept in perfect peace and I am free from evil imaginations promoting lust and demonic inspired cravings in Jesus Name.

9) I claim renewal and continual victory over all destructive appetites and the behavior associated with them.

10) Deliverance from people, places and activities that inspired demonic cravings comes to me in Jesus Name.

CHAPTER 23

DELIVERANCE FROM THE VIOLENT MAN

Psalm 140:1 KJV
***Deliver me from the evil man: and preserve me
from the violent man.***

1) I renounce all generational assignments that breed violence and stir up violent men against me in Jesus Name.

2) Every bloodthirsty demon rooted in the soils of my region, I bind you in Jesus Name.

3) I declare You Lord have arisen in my life and the violent man is scattered and broken in pieces in Jesus name.

4) All conspiracies of violence that are being conjured against my physical well-being and that of my family, the burning and destruction of the Lord come upon you in Jesus Name.

5) Angelic encirclements prevail for me and my household during the day and night in Jesus Name.

6) Plots of violent intrusions, burglaries and thefts during the night are foiled and fail miserably in Jesus Name.

7) I loose havoc and confusion upon all demonic stalkers seeking to mark my steps, daily activities and patterns, demons bent on causing physical harm and bodily injury to me and my family in Jesus Name.

8) The mean and the angry man bent on fostering works of violence shall not come nigh my dwelling.

9) I prophesy the shadow of the Almighty ministering peace and tranquility over my entire realm and sphere of influence.

10) Vials of judgment and swords of justice are loosed against every stronghold and strongman of violence seeking to harm me and my loved ones in Jesus Name.

11) All demonic provocations to stir acts of violence against me, I command to marinate in the blood of Jesus.

12) The blood of Jesus is upon every access point to my physical person and place of dwelling and the violent man is neutralized and forbidden access in Jesus Name.

CHAPTER 24

DEALING WITH FAMILY SPIRITS

Leviticus 19:31 KJV
Regard not them that have familiar spirits,
neither seek after wizards, to be defiled by them:
I am the Lord your God.

1) Lord I repent of all sins of familiarity I've partook of and that of my family in Jesus Name.

2) Any doors open through necromancy, séances, mediums and ceremonies to consult the dead I command closed.

3) Any and all connections to the underworld and hell I decree are cut off and destroyed by fire in Jesus Name.

4) Lord release a purging and cleaning in my family line and deal with all familiar spirits in Jesus Name.

5) I renounce, all psychic and clairvoyant strongmen rooted in familiarity in Jesus Name.

6) Every voice released by demons that would seek to mimic family members who have died are forbidden from speaking into my hearing or communicating with me in my dreams, you devils are bound in Jesus Name.

7) Lord heal me from all affects of familiarity in Jesus Name.

8) All familiar cycles, patterns and occurrences promoting failure, lack, infirmity, resistance towards the things of God is bound in the Name of Jesus.

9) Lord You alone are my source for insight, revelation and knowledge.

10) Every affect of familiarity that has caused me to be restricted in worship, serving, giving and walking in covenant I renounce you I come out of agreement with your hold on my life. I command it to break in Jesus Name.

CHAPTER 25

OPEN HEAVENS

Luke 3:21 KJV
Now when all the people were baptized, it came to pass that Jesus also being baptized and praying the heaven was opened.

1) I decree I live and walk under an open heaven.

2) As Elijah prayed and the heavens opened and released the rains, I decree that through my intercession the rain of You Spirit upon my life subdues all droughts and breaks all famines in Jesus Name.

3) I decree the heavens above me and over my family declare the righteousness of God. Every voice of wickedness above me is rooted out in Jesus Name.

4) Every throne of iniquity above me comes down. Lord Your throne reigns supreme in the heavens.

5) I decree the heavens drop down and the Lord of abundance manifest Himself in the midst.

6) Creativity, inspiration, cunning works and witty ideas empower me to flourish under open heavens.

7) I command a shaking of foundations of darkness established in my life. Lord cause the heaves to drop at Your presence in my life.

8) I decree my eyes shall remain upon the One who legislates in the heavens and orchestrates the plans of earth.

9) My mouth is filled with accurate words and utterances to establish the plans of The Most High.

10) Lord You have put Your words in my mouth and the shadow of Your hand covers me. With Your words I plant the heavens above and by Your words the foundation for Kingdom advancement is laid in the earth.

CHAPTER 26

BANDS OF WICKEDNESS

Isaiah 58:6 KJV
Is not this the fast that I have chosen? To loose the bands of wickedness, to undo heavy burdens and to let the oppressed go free and that ye break every yoke?

1) I renounce every bloodline and societal band of wickedness assigned against my life.

2) Every band of wickedness assigned against my mind to manipulate my destiny and overwhelm me with pressure is broken in the Name of Jesus.

3) Lord as You delivered Israel from Egypt and broke the bands of their yokes so let it be unto me. Every band of the world (Egypt) is broken asunder.

4) Supernatural strength is surging through me and every band rooted in demonic vices is burst asunder. I loose myself from Samson in Jesus Name.

5) All bands of infirmity imposed upon me by witchcraft and bloodline strongholds break in Jesus Name.

6) I decree You redeem my life from death and bring me out of darkness. The bands are now broken asunder.

7) Redemptive power flows through me and restoration from bands of wickedness employed to rob me of my inheritance.

8) I renounce the bands of all mockers sent against me to interfere with destiny in Jesus Name.

9) A renewed grace to fast and consecrate is upon me. Heavy burdens and bands propagating wickedness are destroyed.

10) I am loosed from all bands of control and manipulation imposed upon me by the will of others. I decree I shall not be bound in Jesus Name.

CHAPTER 27

DETHRONING JEZEBEL

Revelation 2:20 KJV
Notwithstanding I have a few things against thee, because thou sufferest that woman Jezebel, which calleth herself a prophetess, to teach and to seduce my servants to commit fornication, and to eat things sacrificed unto idols.

1) I declare the spirit of Jezebel and all minions are dethroned and rendered ineffective in my life.

2) The anointing that was upon Jehu now descends upon me for divine commands to dethrone this wicked spirit in Jesus Name.

3) I command every demonic tower serving as a platform for Jezebel to herald her voice in my sphere to come down in Jesus Name.

4) Every employment of demonic henchmen connected to Jezebel at work to defile and destroy my inheritance through seduction is burned with eternal fire in Jesus Name.

5) All devices of mockery and slander working through the spirit of Jezebel to minimize my progression as a saint is bound.

6) I renounce the sons of Belial and all rumors and accusations released to destroy my credibility and influence as a ministry gift in Jesus Name.

7) Lord cause the influences and the provoking of wickedness manifesting through Jezebel to come to naught in Jesus Name.

8) Every spirit of doctrinal error and deception working through Jezebel to beguile me into erroneous activity is cut off. I sever any lines, cords and connections and renounce you in Jesus Name.

9) Idolatry and personality worship is rooted out and rendered sterile and impotent in Jesus Name.

10) I decree an elevation of my praise and worship unto the You Lord as a means of dethroning the spirit of Jezebel.

11) Every seat and exalted position of Jezebel against my calling and prophetic destiny is overturned and brought low in Jesus Name.

12) Dishonor and demon cohorts working with Jezebel to discredit and devalue ministry gifts and those who have gone before me, I bind you in Jesus Name.

13) Every contract of Jezebel against my marriage, mantle, mission and mandate to seduce me through worldly riches and fame among men is neutralized through the blood of Jesus Christ.

14) I decree double torment, double sorrow, widowhood, plagues of destruction, mourning and famine prevail against the stronghold of Jezebel in the Name of Jesus.

15) All sorcery, witchcraft and lust working with Jezebel to cause defilement and minimize my impact are cut off in Jesus Name.

CHAPTER 28

THE BLESSINGS

Deuteronomy 11:26-27
Behold I set before you this day a blessing and a curse; 27 A blessing, if you obey the commandments of the Lord your God this day.

1) Today I choose to obey and I choose the blessing in Jesus Name.

2) Every curse sent against me to alter my destiny and cloud my judgment ceases in Jesus Name.

3) The blessing is active and operating in every area of my life.

4) I decree the blessing makes me rich and causes me to excel, exceeding in life and no sorrow is added to me.

5) Power for productivity, wisdom for success and opulence are upon me because of the blessing.

6) Every mentality and system of lack are divinely restricted from my life because of the blessing.

7) I receive a divine shift in my mind, character and nature by the blessing of the Lord.

8) New frontiers, new options, new doors, new connections, new favor, new money, new peace, new platforms, new things flow abundantly by Your blessing upon my life.

9) I decree the blessing of the Lord empowers me to walk right before and continually honor His word.

10) Ability to be fruitful, productive, multiple, expand, subdue, conquer, replenish, restore, dominate and govern in my sphere are increasing because of the blessings.

11) A good name is to be desired above great riches and by the blessing of the Lord I decree my name is made great in the earth.

12) Commanded blessings are upon my storehouse, investments, savings, retirement funds and all monetary resources in Jesus Name.

13) By Your blessings I have wisdom and discipline to live debt free; cycles of debt are broken and I'm loosed from every oppressive creditor in Jesus Name.

14) By Your blessing I prosper in all assignments, business endeavors and exploits I put my hands to.

15) I have liberation from financial ruin, relationship despair, social injustice and generational proclivities by the blessing of the Lord.

CHAPTER 29

THE KINGDOM

Psalm 103:19 KJV
The Lord hath prepared his throne in the heavens; and his kingdom ruleth over all.

1) I renounce any known and unknown allegiances to any other kingdom and repent of knowingly or unknowingly yielding to any other gods in Jesus Name.

2) Your Kingdom is my priority and I decree the King of this Kingdom rules and reigns on the throne of my life.

3) Grace and capacity abound in me to press into Your Kingdom.

4) Deliverances from generational powers interfering with Kingdom exploits are overthrown and rendered ineffective in Jesus Name.

5) Lord arise upon Your throne of fire and loose Your eternal burning upon every stronghold or darkness over my life in Jesus Name.

6) I command thrones of iniquity to be dismantle over my life for Your throne is exalted in the heavens and Your Kingdom rules over all.

7) Every governing force of darkness loosed against my destiny is brought low because the Kingdom is the Lords and You rule over all.

8) Lord from Your throne release deliverance unto me and cause every demonic legislation and enactment of darkness summoned against me to experience utter ruin in Jesus Name.

9) I decree Your Kingdom consumes and breaks in pieces every other Kingdom. I prophesy consumption and breaking upon the powers of witchcraft, poverty, deception, lust, rebellion, pride, rejection, delusion, instability, fear, intimidation and python spirits in Jesus Name.

10) I receive a fresh impartation of grace to speak of Your Kingdom and talk of Your power. I declare that through my life the glorious majesty of Your Kingdom shall be made known throughout all the earth.

CHAPTER 30

COMMANDING YOUR DAY

Job 38:12-13 KJV
Hast thou commanded the morning since thy days; and caused the dayspring to know his place; 13 That it might take hold of the ends of the earth, that the wicked might be shaken out of it?

1) As a king in the earth I declare divine sentences flow from my lips and I command order, increase and breakthrough over my day.

2) I speak to every power working against the success and progression of my day. These devils are bound in Jesus Name.

3) I decree open portals over myself and family. The provisions and glory of my King is released in our lives.

4) A new day has dawned upon me so cause the release of a fresh anointing to manifest upon me in Jesus Name.

5) As the mornings released fresh manna unto Your people, Israel, let it be unto me. Fresh insights, fresh revelations and fresh impartations fall upon me in Jesus Name.

6) I command every wicked strategy forged in the night against my mandate to be shaken out of its position.

7)   Every confederacy of evil bent on ruining my day and invoking havoc on my family is bound and neutralized by the blood of Jesus Christ.

8)   Lord send forth Your Spirit, Light and Truth to organize and direct the affairs of my day in Jesus Name.

9)   I command all advocates of mayhem, chaos and confusion to be displaced from my day.

10) Everything that can be shaken shall be shaken, I prophesy a shaking in the heavens over my life and all seeds planted that have their origin in darkness are rooted out and crop failure prevails in Jesus Name.

CHAPTER 31

ACTIVATING THE ANGELIC REALM

Psalm 103:20 KJV
Bless the Lord, ye his angels, that excel in strength, that do his commandments, hearkening unto the voice of his word.

1) I declare an activation of the host of heaven on my behalf. Those messengers and agents of fire who excel in strength and hearken to the voice of Your word come forth in Jesus Name.

2) I decree the angel of the Lord encamps around me and I enjoy encirclements of angelic power in Jesus Name.

3) I decree Your angels have charge over my life and they keep me in the ways of You, the Sovereign One.

4) Supernatural provisions are ministered unto me by the angelic forces dispatched by heaven on my behalf.

5) Lord activate those spirit beings, even Your angels ordained to provide deliverance and breakthrough for me to come forward in Jesus Name.

6) I declare every tactical delay to heavenly mandates being fulfilled in my life break and angelic assistance prevails in Jesus Name.

7) Lord as angels were dispatched to strengthen You after battling the forces of darkness, let them be sent to strengthen me.

8) Every temptation that's common to man, I overcome as the Lord Himself and His angels are also preserving me.

9) Lord activate those from the angelic realm that You have sent to provide protection for me and my family.

10) I receive the ministry of angels sent by God into my realm who appear as strangers.

CHAPTER 32

SOUL DESTROYERS

Psalm 40:14 KJV
Let them be ashamed and confounded together that seek after my soul to destroy it; let them be driven backward and put to shame that wish me evil.

1) Lord forgive me of any sins I've committed and those family members, before me, who have opened my lineage to soul destroyers and wasters.

2) I renounce every vice and stronghold legally intact that serves as a catalyst for spirits of darkness to hunt my soul.

3) Lord cause confusion and strong delusion to manifest against every destroyer deployed against my soul in Jesus Name.

4) Every evil and cruel messenger sent against my soul to defile it, I renounce you in Jesus Name.

5) I disallow and loose failure into all rebellion seeking to drive me to a life of insubordination and defilement to my soul.

6) I command rejection, insecurity and identity issues that would seek to breach my soul to come out of me and go in Jesus Name.

7) I decree I am accepted in the Beloved and all soul hunters and destroyers working to unnerve me are defeated in Jesus Name.

8) All emotional schemes and mind manipulating agencies working to destabilize my soul are rooted out and burned by the fire of God.

9) I renounce all panic, dread and anxieties stirred by soul destroyers deployed to undermine my future and make a mockery of my life in Jesus Name.

10) No weapon or works formed against my soul shall prosper for the Lord stands up for me and declares that He is my salvation.

CHAPTER 33

SUCCESS BREAKTHROUGHS

Genesis 39:3-4 NIV
When his master saw that the LORD was with him and that the LORD gave him success in everything he did, 4 Joseph found favor in his eyes and became his attendant. Potiphar put him in charge of his household and entrusted to his care everything he owned.

1) Lord as Potiphar acknowledged You were with Joseph, I declare the Potiphar's of my day shall do likewise unto me. I decree success and favor over every endeavor I put my hands to in Jesus Name.

2) I decree every stalemate to my progress and success is divinely displaced and overtaken in Jesus Name.

3) I prophesy new realms of discipline over my life in the area of preparation for successful exploits. All time wasters are neutralized and driven out in Jesus Name.

4) Tangible displays of Your presence prevail on my behalf granting me favor and continued success.

5) Lord grant me the wisdom to develop structure in my life inspired by You to bring forth success in all You've ordained for me to advance Your Kingdom.

6) I decree that as I meditate upon Your word day and night You make my way prosperous and I enjoy good success.

7) Lord as I observe Your commandments and honor Your statues, cause heavens agenda for me to thrive, succeed and manifest like a flowing river.

8) Every plot to foil my mandate and mission for success is undermined and rendered obsolete.

9) Father calibrate my mind for greater and the success that You've planned for me. I decree accuracy in my thinking and perception in Jesus Name.

10) I decree strategic and calculated thinking emerges in me to execute from start to finish plans and ideas given to me for success.

CHAPTER 34

OVERCOMING BARRIERS AND PROGRESSION BLOCKERS

2 Samuel 22:30 KJV
For by Thee have I run through a troop: by my God have I leaped over a wall.

1) Lord empower me to breakthrough all demonic troops positioned to hinder me from moving forward in purpose and leaping into my next level.

2) Every barrier to my progress and advancement, I triumph over in Jesus Name.

3) I renounce all barriers assigned against my mind established to prohibit me from receiving ideas and acquiring knowledge.

4) Strength to progress relationally and develop healthy paradigms for bonding with others is upon me.

5) Grace to excel and triumph over every economic barrier abounds within me in Jesus Name.

6) Wisdom to overcome and navigate demonic landmines surges in my life.

7) I thrive with divine insight and internal fortitude to champion over social injustice barriers in Jesus Name.

8) Lord strengthen me to properly dispose of every barrier opposing me from progressing and growing as a believer.

9) All barriers of pride, confusion, mental blocks and mind binding spirits; the Lord rebuke you.

10) Every spiritual barrier rooted in offense designed to trap and cause me to stumble; I decree power is upon me to rise above you in Jesus Name.

CHAPTER 35

THE VOICE OF THE LORD

Psalm 29:3
The voice of the Lord is upon the waters: the God of glory thundereth: the Lord is upon many waters.

1)   Lord cause Your voice to be amplified and thunder throughout my mandate and sphere.

2)   The voice of the LORD renders every demonic force conspiring against impotent and ineffective in Jesus Name.

3)   Every cycle of injustice and unjust works pressuring me to compromise are broken asunder by the voice of the LORD.

4)   I decree glory and power for breakthrough manifest in me by the voice of the LORD.

5)   The threats and intimidations of darkness are neutralized and overthrown by the voice of the LORD.

6)   Strongholds and strongmen are divinely displaced from my destiny as the voice of the LORD roars over me.

7)   My ears are awakened, my tongue is disciplined and the LORD utters His voice through me.

8) I declare new realms of majesty and power manifest in my life by the voice of the LORD.

9) The fiery plans of darkness and the forces of the underworld receive strong derision and confusion by the voice of the LORD.

10) Intangibles are breaking forth in my life by the voice of the LORD. Every resource necessary for this season is searching me out for the voice of the LORD is summoning them now.

MORE GREAT RESOURCES FROM
Stephen A. Garner Ministries

Books

- Apostolic Pioneering
- Benefits of Praying in Tongues
- Exposing the Spirit of Anger
- Fundamentals of Deliverance 101, Revised and Expanded
- Pray Without Ceasing, Special Edition
- Restoring Prophetic Watchmen
- Deliver Us From Evil
- Essentials of the Prophetic Revised & Expanded
- The Kingdom of God: A Believer's Guide to Kingdom Living
- Kingdom Prayer
- Prayers, Decrees and Confessions for Wisdom
- Prayers, Decrees and Confessions for Favour & Grace
- Prayers, Decrees and Confessions for Prosperity
- Prayers, Decrees and Confessions for Increase
- Prayers, Decrees and Confessions for Righteousness
- Prayers, Decrees and Confessions for Goodness & Mercy
- Prayers. Decrees and Confessions for Power
- Prayers, Decrees and Confessions for Rewards
- Prayers, Decrees and Confessions for Peace
- Prayers, Decrees and Confessions for Healing
- Prayers that Strengthen Marriages and Families
- Strife The Enemy of Advancement

CD's

- Prayers For The Nations
- Prayers Against Python & Witchcraft
- Prayers of Healing & Restoration
- Prayers of Renunciation and Deliverance
- Thy Kingdom Come
- The Glory
- Overcoming Spirits of Terrorism
- The Spirit of the Breaker
- The Fear of The Lord

CONTACT INFORMATION
STEPHEN A. GARNER MINISTRIES
P.O. BOX 1545, BOLINGBROOK, IL 60440
EMAIL: SAGARNERMINISTRIES@GMAIL.COM
WWW.SAGMINISTRIES.COM

Made in the USA
Lexington, KY
10 November 2019